# PRAYER HAS POWER TO GET RESULTS!

## *A BOOK OF PRAYERS*

## GENOLIA HOLMES

Treasured Word Publishing

PRAYER HAS POWER TO GET RESULTS!
A BOOK OF PRAYERS

© 2020 by Genolia Holmes

Library of Congress Control Number: 2020925431

ISBN:      Softcover    978-1-7363505-0-8

           EBook        978-1-7363505-1-5

All Scripture quotations, unless otherwise indicated are taken from the King James Version. All rights reserved.

Printed in the United States of America.

Cover Design: Sam Smith

Editor: John Eger

This book was printed in the United States of America.

# DEDICATION

To my Facebook Group: Prayer Warriors

And to my inner circle - Prayer Sister:

Rachel Villarreal

And all of my sisters in JOY Prayer Warriors Group

Thank you for praying for me and for the publication

of this book.

I love you all.

*If you worry, you are a worrier.*
*If you pray, you are a Warrior!*

# ACKNOWLEDEMENTS

A special thanks to

My Facebook Mentors:

Tamara Mitchell-Davis and Leah M. Forney
Writer's Community for Women

You have helped me to stay on task and to be accountable during the writing of this book. You have pushed me to finish what I've started. Thank you.

I appreciate all that you ladies do, my sister writers.

# Table of Contents

# INTRODUCTION

You can change your life by the words that you speak, I want to show you how in this book. There is a solution for every problem that you are dealing with. The Bible is filled with many prayers and in this book, I want to share with you some of the first prayers that I prayed and still pray today. I want to share with you how these prayers have transformed my life and how they can do the same for you. God's Word is always your main course, a spiritual meal, and this book is like a gummy supplement (sweet and effective) that you can chew on as you're rushing through your busy life. As you pray these prayers out loud your faith will be built by the words you hear. If you have faith to believe, then you will see and experience results for you and for loved ones. You may not be able to carry your Bible around with you in public places, but you can carry this book with you and refer to it often when you are dealing with battles in your life. Expect to see results because prayer produces results!

# PART 1:

# PERSONAL

# PRAYERS

> "The heartfelt and persistent prayer
> of the righteous believer has great power and
> produces wonderful results."
>
> James 5:16

# Say It Loud!

*"Faith comes by hearing, and hearing by the Word of God."*

*Romans 10:17*

Since faith comes by hearing, your faith increases when the right things are heard. If you read God's Word silently then you can't hear what you're reading. Faith comes by hearing! So when you are reading God's Word – read aloud!

When you pray, pray aloud! Begin by placing your hand on your heart and sit in silence for a few moments. Be still, without movement for a moment to hear what God is saying to you, His Spirit speaking to your spirit – *"a gentle whisper"* (1st Kings 19:12). Sometimes we are doing too much and don't take necessary moments to pause and seek direction from God. We look to everyone else to tell us what we should do, but He wants us to come into a quiet place of prayer.

> *Jesus said, "Therefore I say to you, whatever things you ask when you pray, believe that you receive them, and you will have them."*
>
> Mark 11:24

# Your Secret Place

Jesus teaches how to prepare ourselves before we offer up our prayers.

*"When you pray, don't be like the hypocrites. They love to stand in the synagogues and on the street corners and pray loudly. They want people to see them. The truth is, that's all the reward they will get. But when you pray, you should go into your room and close the door. Then pray to your Father. He is there in that private place. He can see what is done in private, and He will reward you.*

*And when you pray, don't be like the people who don't know God. They say the same things again and again. They think they will be heard because or their many words. Don't be like them. Your Father knows what you need before you ask Him."*

Matthew 6:5-8

Prayer is a privilege! We get to pray to the Holy One, Creator of all, our heavenly Father. Although He knows you better than you know yourself, He invites you (one of His many creations) into His presence to talk to Him. That's a powerful thought! Coming into His presence gives you power.

Prayer is the catalyst that changed my life. I remember days when I would get up before everyone else. It was still dark outside, and I would drag myself out of bed only to fall asleep on my knees beside my bed. I kept getting up until I was finally able to pray without falling asleep. Slowly things began to change in my life but, most importantly, things began to change in me. Things that once made me angry didn't bother me anymore. I was able to smile through things that once caused me pain or sorrow. I was able to forgive people that I would have cursed out before. My complaining turned into gratitude. It's a process and it does not happen overnight. The same transformation can happen in your life. When people say, "prayer changes things!" It's true. The change will start with you.

# The First Thing

If someone gave you this book or you have come across this book, it's not by coincidence. I want you to get the full benefit of this book. So if you don't know the God to whom I'm referring to in this book, I want to start by introducing Him. It's only through a personal relationship with Him that you can pray the prayers in this book and get results in your life. He is the God that hears and answers prayer.

Pray this simple prayer or one similar to this one, and say it aloud and believe in your heart the words of this prayer:

Heavenly Father, I know that I am a sinner. I believe that Jesus Christ, Your Son, died on the cross for my sins and rose from the dead to be my Lord. God, I ask you to forgive me for all of the wrong things that I have done. I repent of my sins and I invite Jesus into my heart. I ask that you cleanse me. Thank you, Jesus for giving me the free gift of eternal life. I promise to live for You as You reveal Yourself to me through Your Word, the Holy Bible. I ask that You fill me with Your Holy Spirit. In Jesus name, I pray. Amen.

> *"Most assuredly, I say to you, unless one is born again,*
> *he cannot see the kingdom of God."*
> John 3:3

# The ABC's
# Accept - Believe - Confess

**1. Admit that you have done wrong and ask God to forgive you.**

*"For all have sinned and fall short of the glory of God."*
   Romans 3:23

**2. Believe that Jesus Christ died on the cross and rose again as repayment for your sin.**

*"Believe on the Lord Jesus Christ, and you will be saved."*
*Acts 16:31*

*"For God so loved the world, that He gave His only begotten Son, that whosoever believes in Him should not perish, but have everlasting life."*

*John 3:16*

### 3. **Confess that you believe in Jesus Christ.**

*If you **openly say**, "Jesus is Lord" and believe in your heart that God raised him from death, you will be saved.*

*Believe in Jesus deep in your hearts, so that you are made right with God. And openly say that you believe in him, and you are saved.*

*Romans 10:9-10*

# The Cross

A symbol of my faith
That strengthens me each day
By God's grace I walk in the narrow way.

You see God's own Son
He gave His life for me
And took my debt of sin to a place called Calvary.

I owe Him my life
And all I'll ever be
All He asks is that I let Him live through me.

So I run the race
Empowered by His grace
And give Him all the glory as I look into His face.

JESUS is LORD!

Author Unknown

# The Model Prayer

*JESUS said to pray like this:*

*Our Father, Which Art In Heaven,*

*Hallowed Be Thy Name.*

(Our Father, in heaven, Holy is Your Name)

This is adoration for your Heavenly Father, and you are

making known to Him your love for Him.

*Your Kingdom Come, Lord*

(May Your Kingdom come soon)

This is divine intervention.

*Your Will Be Done, Lord*

(May Your will be done in my life, as it is in heaven)

This is showing submission to God.

*Give Us This Day Our Daily Bread*

(Give me today the food I need, both physically and spiritually)

This is provision because He is your Provider.

Forgive Us Our Debts, As We Forgive our Debtors

(Forgive me of the sins that I've committed,

and help me to forgive those who have sinned against me)

You must forgive others so that you will be forgiven.


*Lead Us Not Into Temptation, But Deliver Us From Evil*

(Don't let me yield to temptation, but rescue me from the evil

one)

You are thanking God for His Guidance and Deliverance.


*For Thine is the Kingdom*

*and the Power,*

*and the Glory, Forever*

(Yours is the Kingdom and the power and the glory, eternally)


*Matthew 6:9-13*

# Choose Life!

*"Today I am giving you a choice of two ways. And I ask heaven and earth to be witnesses of your choice. You can choose life or death. The first choice will bring a blessing. The other choice will bring a curse. So choose life! Then you and your children will live."*

*Deuteronomy 30:19 ERV*

God has given each of us free will. You get to choose how you want to live your life. You can choose life in Christ Jesus or you can choose the ways of the world that lead to destruction. The decision is yours!

I want to encourage you to seek God, choose to read, believe and speak His Word. His Word is the Holy Bible. The words in the Bible can transform your thinking and can put you on the right path. This book that you hold in your hand is actually a tool that is intended to draw you closer to God. The life that you choose not only affects you, it affects everyone connected to you.

All of us have pressures to deal with in life. How will you choose in the middle of pressure? Life (Blessing and Faith)? Or will you choose death (Curses and Feelings)? You always have a choice.

> *Jesus said to him, "I am the way, the truth, and the life. No one comes to the Father except through Me."*
>
> John 14:6

# A Winning Strategy

*"Seek first the Kingdom of God above all else, and live righteously, and He will give you everything you need."*
*Matthew 6:33*

Be determined to set the path for your prayer life every day.

Prayer is simply a conversation with God.

You talk to Him and He speaks to you through His Word.

Prayer is a dialogue – not a monologue. You don't do all of the talking; God wants to talk as well. That's why it's so important to keep the Holy Bible near you during your prayer time. You may also want to bring a notebook and pen.

No prayer – no power

Little prayer – little power

More prayer – more power

Start your day with prayer and God will give you some key insight and revelation. Challenge yourself to get up thirty minutes to an hour before you go to work. Do you want to receive strategies for your day? Then do something that you've never done so that you can receive things that you only dream of. Your days at work can become stress free over time. More prayer – more power!

# You are loved

*"Give all your worries and cares to God, for He cares about you."*

1ˢᵗ Peter 5:7

If you have never felt loved by anyone else, then I want to start out by telling you that Christ Jesus loves you. He loves you so much that He suffered, bled, and died for you. The Holy Bible is a book of life for you. Its not an ancient book for past generations; it's for you right here and right now! God cares about you!

This book is filled with personalized prayers because God is a personal God. You are special to Him and He longs to have a personal relationship with you. People disappoint us sometimes, they are limited in their ability to love and can be quite fickle. But God is always there, even when you don't feel Him or see Him working on your behalf. He's there always.

*God says, "I will never leave you; I will never run away from you."*

*So we can feel sure and say, "The Lord is my Helper; I will not be afraid."*

*Hebrews 13:5-6 ERV*

One of the things that amaze me is God's capacity for detail. There are billions of people on planet earth, but yet He knows each of His children intimately. He looks at the heart and He knows the thoughts we have. He even knows how many hairs are on your head, if you have hair ☺

*"And the very hairs on your head are all numbered. So don't be afraid; you are more valuable to God than a whole flock of sparrows."*

*Luke 12:7*

# Prayer of Protection

(Personalized – say this aloud daily)


*I live in the shelter of the Most High*
*And I find rest in the shadow of the Almighty.*


*This I declare about the LORD:*
*He alone is my refuge, my place of safety;*
*He is my God, and I trust Him.*


*For He rescues me from every trap*
*and He protects me from deadly diseases.*


*He covers me with His feathers.*
*He shelters me with His wings.*
*His faithful promises are my armor and protection.*


*I am not afraid of the terror of the night,*
*Nor the arrow that flies in the day.*

*I will not dread the disease that stalks in darkness,*
*Nor the disaster that strikes at midday.*

*Though a thousand may fall at my side,*
*Though ten thousand are dying around me,*
*These evils will not touch me.*

*I will just open my eyes ,*
*And see how the wicked are punished.*

*The LORD is my refuge,*
*and the LORD Most High is my shelter,*

*No evil will conquer me;*
*No plague will come near my home.*

*The LORD orders His angels*
*to protect me wherever I go.*

*They hold me up with their hands,*
*So I won't even hurt my foot on a stone.*

*I trample upon lions and cobras;*
*I crush fierce lions and serpents under my feet!*

*The LORD rescues me, I love Him!*
*He protects me, I trust in His name.*

*When I call on the LORD, He answers me;*
*He is with me in trouble.*
*He will rescue me and He will honor me.*

*He will reward me with a long life*
*And He will give me His salvation.*

*Psalm 91*

*NLT*

*"For God has not given us a spirit of fear, but of power and of love and of a sound mind."*
2nd Timothy 1:7

# Assurance of God's help

*Fear not, for I am with you;*

*Be not dismayed, for I am your God.*

*I will strengthen you,*

*Yes, I will help you,*

*I will uphold you with my righteous right hand*

Isaiah 41:10


*"Jesus Christ is the same yesterday, today, and forever."*

*Hebrews 13:8*

# A Blessed Day!

Your words create your reality!

*I speak to this brand new day and I call this day blessed because*

*This is the day the LORD has made. I rejoice and I'm glad in it.*
Psalm 118:24

*I praise You, O LORD, with my whole heart.*
Psalm 9:1

*Your Word is a lamp unto my feet, and a light unto my path.*
*Thank You for Your Word, O LORD.*
Psalm 119:105

*I will bless You, LORD, at all times: and Your praise will continually be in my mouth.*

Psalm 34:1


*Thank You, Heavenly Father for supplying all of my needs according to Your riches in glory by Christ Jesus.*

Philippians 4:19


*Thank You LORD, I praise You – great is Your faithfulness toward me and my family. Thank You LORD, that Your mercies are new to us every morning.*

Lamentations 3: 22-23


*I trust in You LORD, with all my heart, and I will not depend on my own understanding. In all my ways, I acknowledge You!*
*Thank You LORD, for directing my steps and showing me which paths to take.*

Proverbs 3:6

*I can do all things through Christ Jesus who strengthens me.*

Philippians 4:13


*The joy of the LORD is my strength!*

Nehemiah 8:10


*Thank You, LORD, for giving me wisdom in every area of my life.*

James 1:5


*You have not given me a spirit of fear; You have given me power, love, and a sound mind. Thank You, LORD!*

2<sup>ND</sup> Timothy 1:7


*Let the words of my mouth, and the meditation of my heart, be acceptable in Your sight, O LORD, my strength, and my redeemer.*

Psalm 19:14

*LORD, set a guard over my mouth, and keep watch over the door of my lips. Let no corrupt communication proceed out of my mouth.*

Psalm 141:3 and Ephesians 4:29

*No weapon formed against me shall prosper, and every tongue that rises against me in judgment will be condemned.*

Isaiah 54:17

*I am the redeemed of the LORD, and I will say so, for Jesus has redeemed me from the hand of the enemy.*

Psalm 107:2

*I am blessed in the city and I am blessed in the field. I'm blessed coming in and I'm blessed going out. Wherever I go and whatever I do is blessed of the LORD.*

Deuteronomy 28:3,6

In JESUS Name I pray. Amen.

"And you shall remember the LORD your God, for it is He who gives you power to get wealth."

Deuteronomy 8:18

# According to Your Faith

Make these powerful declarations every day! Say them  aloud.

Speak & Hear God's Word!

*I set the course of my life with my declarations.*
James 3:5

*My prayers are powerful and effective.*
James 5:16b

*God richly supplies all my financial needs.*
Philippians 4:19

*I am dead to sin and alive to obeying God.*
Romans 6:11

*I walk in divine health.*
Isaiah 53:5

*I live under a supernatural protection.*
Psalm 91

*I consistently bring God encounters to other people.*
Mark 16:17

*Each of my family members is wonderfully blessed and loves Jesus.*
Acts 16:31

*God is on my side; therefore I cannot be defeated, discouraged, depressed, or disappointed.*
Romans 8:37

*I am the head and not the tail. I have insight and I have wisdom.*
*I have authority in Christ Jesus.*
Deuteronomy 28:13
*I speak to the raging waters in my life: peace, be still.*

*I say to my mind; peace, be still.*

*I say to my emotions; peace, be still.*

*I say to my body; peace, be still.*

*I say to my home; peace, be still.*

*I say to my family; peace, be still.*

Mark 4:39

*As I speak God's promises, they come to pass.*
*They stop all attacks, assaults, oppression, and fear from my life.*
*I speak to every mountain of fear, every mountain of discouragement, every mountain of stress, every mountain*

*of depression, every mountain of lack and insufficiency; and*

*I say,*

*"Be removed and cast into the sea in Jesus' Name!"*

Mark 11:22-24


*I have the wisdom of God today. I will think the right*
*thoughts, say the right words, and make the right decisions*
*in every situation I face.*

James 1:5

*I expect the best day of my life spiritually, emotionally,*
*relationally, and financially in Jesus' Name.*

Romans 15:13

# A Prayer to Comfort You

Many of us are accustomed to hearing this prayer read when we lose a loved one, but I have found this prayer to be one that you can say out loud often, because truly the Lord is our Shepherd. He is not just a shepherd; the Bible says He's the Good Shepherd. He cares for you.  He provides for you, and He guides you everyday – if you are willing to follow His lead. Even if you have been labeled the "black sheep" of the family, Jesus will still care for and comfort you as well. He cares for all sheep and He's not concerned about the outer appearance of the sheep. His love for you is unconditional.

*Jesus said, "I am the good shepherd: the good shepherd gives His life for the sheep."*

John 10:11

Comfort yourself today with God's Word …

*The LORD is my Shepherd* – that's relationship with God.

*I shall not want* – He supplies everything that you need.

*He makes me lie down in green pastures* – He gives you rest.

*He leads me beside still waters* – that's refreshment for your soul.

*He leads me in the paths of righteousness* – He guides you.

*For His name's sake* – He has a specific purpose for your life.

*When I walk through the valley of the shadow of death* – this is a time of testing.

*I will fear no evil* – know that God is your protection.

*For God is with me* – you are faithful in knowing that He will never leave you.

*His rod and His staff, they comfort me* – that's discipline for you.

*God prepares a table before me in the presence of my enemies* – your hope is in the Lord.

*God anoints my head with oil* – that's consecration.

*My cup runs over* – that's abundance.

*Surely goodness and mercy will follow me all the days of my life* – that's blessing.

*And I will dwell in the house of the LORD* – that's security.

*Forever* – that's eternity.

Psalm 23

# Sheep need the Good Shepherd

Throughout Scripture, people are frequently referred

to as sheep.

Look at:

Psalms 79:13; 95:7; 100:3

Isaiah 53:6

Jeremiah 50:6

Ezekiel 34:17-22

Micah 2:12

Matthew 9:36; 10:16

John 21:15-17

One characteristic of sheep is that they tend to wander and are incapable of taking care of themselves. They need a shepherd to guide them to pasture and to protect them from predators and thieves. Yet throughout the Bible we also see that sheep were highly valued. They provided food and clothing for people and sacrifices to the temple. Sheep know their shepherd and respond to the shepherd's voice. The Good Shepherd – Jesus – calls His sheep individually by name and He leads them.

Just like sheep, you may tend to wander away from the Shepherd when trials, tribulations, and tests come your way. These things come in the form of the death of a loved one or could also be personal traumas in your life such as financial ruin, relationship difficulties, or prolonged sickness and disease. You keep asking, "Why did this happen to me?" And if you have no understanding of what's going on in your life it could be easy, to become angry with God.

When you decide to wander away in anger or discontent you place yourself in danger. The enemy of your soul will deceive you and even lead you to a place of spiritual or physical death. You are valuable to God. Even when you choose to wander away from Him, He will call you and He will pursue you because He loves you. He longs to take good care of you all the days of your life. He knows your name and everything about you.

Luke 15:1-7

Sheep can get their head caught in thorny plants and die trying to get untangled. There are little flies that like to torment sheep by laying eggs in their nostrils that turn into worms and drive the sheep to beat their head against a rock, sometimes to death. Their ears and eyes are susceptible to tormenting insects. So the shepherd anoints their whole head with oil. Then there is peace.

That oil forms a barrier of protection against the insects that try to destroy the sheep. Do you have times of mental torment? Do worrisome thoughts invade your mind over and over? Do you beat your head against a wall trying to stop them? Have you ever asked God to anoint your head with oil?

Our shepherd has an endless supply! His oil protects and makes it possible for you to fix your heart, mind, and eyes on Him today and always! There is peace in the valley! May the Good Shepherd anoint your head with oil today so that your cup overflows with blessings.

# Anointed With Oil

"For the wages of sin is death, but the gift of God is eternal life through Jesus Christ our Lord."
Romans 6:23

Thorny plants can symbolize bad decisions that get you caught up in sin. The trap of sin can tangle you up and cause death. Flies are pesky little creatures that can torment with their annoying presence. They are unclean insects carrying all kinds of disease because they feed on dead things. The eggs that they lay contain nasty maggots and a foul odor follows where flies and maggots exist. They hang out near garbage dumpsters. Your nose is how you discern odor, so the worms are trying to block your ability to discern.

It's been said, "your ears and eyes are gateways to your soul." Over the years I have heard it preached time and time again that you must guard your eyes because lust can enter in through what your eyes see and covet. And you must guard your ears because bad news and murderous gossip can enter in through your ears. It's ironic that the tormenting insects are attacking the eyes and ears of the sheep.

*"But blessed are your eyes, for they see: and your ears, for they hear."*

*Matthew 13:16*

The shepherd anoints the whole head of the sheep; the head must be protected at all times because nothing functions properly without the head. The enemy attacks through your thoughts. If he can control your thoughts, then he can control all of you. Birds fly over your head but you will not allow them to make a nest in your hair; don't allow evil suggestions of the devil to take root in your mind.

*"We can demolish every deceptive fantasy that opposes God and break through every arrogant attitude that is raised up in defiance of the true knowledge of God. We capture, like*

prisoners of war, every thought and insist that it bow in obedience to the Anointed One."

2<sup>nd</sup> Corinthians 10:5

The Good Shepherd is our peace. His very touch and presence are peace. Anointing oil is used throughout the Bible to anoint people and things. It's a point of contact. Allow the good shepherd to anoint you with oil today and every day.

Declare this today: *"I have been anointed with fresh oil."*
*Psalm 92:10*

As a child of God, you have the authority to anoint yourself with oil, anoint your children with oil, and anoint your physical possessions with oil, **only as a point of contact.**

*"But to as many as did receive and welcome Him, He gave the right [the authority, the privilege] to become children of God, that is, to those who believe in (adhere to, trust in, and rely on) His name."*

*John 1:12 AMP*

# Blessed Oil

Oil should be consecrated (blessed) before using it for anointing.

A good quality pure olive oil is good.

1. Hold the open container of oil.

2. Pray this prayer or a similar prayer over the oil: Heavenly Father, by the authority of the Lord Jesus Christ, I consecrate, dedicate and set apart this special oil for anointing anyone, anything at any time for any Christian purpose, and, I do this in the name of the Lord Jesus Christ. Amen.

3. After you have consecrated the oil, keep it in a special place and use it only for the purpose of anointing.

4. When you are using the anointing oil to anoint someone: use a very small amount of oil and

"draw" a cross on the forehead of the person or the object being anointed.

5. Speak the Word of God and pray the word of God. This can also be a time to praise and worship God.

*Jesus said, "If two or three people are together believing in me, I am there with them*

*Matthew 18:20*

# Your New True Identity

*"God created humans in His own image. He created them*

*to be like*

*Himself. He created them male and female."*

*Genesis 1:27*

Your spirit is connected to God's Spirit if you are born again. Although you are not God and you will never be God, you are born into His family when you accept Jesus as your Lord and Savior. Your true identity is found in Christ Jesus, because you are a spirit, you have a soul and you live in a body. Your first and true identity is your spiritual connection to God, not the culture of your physical existence; that's secondary.

Once you know who you are in Christ, you can't keep doing the same things that you did according to your flesh. A change has to occur. Maybe in the past you got drunk and exploded on others, or maybe you were promiscuous and living a life of fornication; all of these behaviors can be transformed in Christ. You can't change them alone; you will need God's help. You will never be perfect, no matter how hard you try. The goal is not perfection the goal is maturity and excellence.

There are many Scriptures in the Bible to assist you in moving toward change, maturity and excellence.

*"If we [freely] admit that we have sinned and confess our sins, He is faithful and just [true to His own nature and promises], and will forgive our sins and cleanse us continually from all unrighteousness [our wrongdoing, everything not in conformity with His will and purpose].*

*1st John 1:9 AMP*

The reality is that when you accept Christ Jesus into your life, you die to your old flesh and your spirit is raised to a new place in Him. You are now connected to a new body that no longer desires the old cravings – a renewal occurs. It is a process, and when you make prayer a vital part of your daily life, the transformation begins and you get stronger and stronger each day. You are now a part of a new family that unities you with other believers all over the world. The spiritual bond is so strong that it tears down racial, ethnic, social class, and national obstacles. In this new family of believers we are designed to work together and to watch out for each other like a team. Teams function best when they work together.

The Apostle Paul uses the metaphor of *taking off* and *putting on* clothing to explain how to live according to your new identity in Jesus. You must *take off* old identities, unpleasant attitudes and unproductive habits and instead *put on* (clothe yourself) through the Holy Spirit with the enduring qualities of your new identity in Christ Jesus.

# New Creation Life

Colossians 3:5-15

*Put to death*, therefore, whatever belongs to your earthly nature: sexual immorality, impurity, lust, evil desires and greed, which is idolatry.

Because of these the wrath of God is coming.

You used to walk in these ways, in the life you once lived.

But now you must also *rid yourselves of* all such things as these: anger, rage, malice, slander, and filthy language from your lips.

Do not lie to each other, since you have **taken off** your old self with its practices.

And have **put on** the new self, which is being renewed in knowledge in the image of its Creator.

In this new creation life, your nationality makes no difference, or your ethnicity, education, or economic status  - they matter nothing. For it is Christ that means everything as He lives in every one of us!

Therefore, as God's chosen people, holy and dearly loved, *clothe yourselves* with compassion, kindness, humility, gentleness, and patience.

Bear with each other and forgive one another if any of you has a grievance against someone. Forgive as the LORD forgave you.

And over all these virtues *put on* love, which binds them all together in perfect unity.

Let the peace of Christ rule in your hearts, since as members of one body you were called to peace. And always be thankful.

# Put Your Clothes On

Ephesians 6:10-18 NLT

Just as you would never leave your house half-dressed, don't go out into the world each day without putting on your spiritual clothing. God gives you something to put on every day to protect you from the battles all around you. When you are putting on your clothes in the natural, make sure you **put on** the whole armor of God.

Be strong in the Lord and in His mighty power.

**Put on** all of God's armor so that you will be able to stand firm against all strategies of the devil.

For you are not fighting against flesh and blood enemies, but against evil rulers and authorities of the unseen world, against mighty powers in this dark world, and against evil spirits in heavenly places.

Therefore, **put on** every piece of God's armor so you will be able to resist the enemy in the time of evil. Then after the battle you will still be standing firm.

Stand your ground, **put on** the belt of truth and the breastplate of God's righteousness.

For shoes, **put on** the peace that comes from the Good News so that you will be fully prepared.

In addition to all these, hold up the shield of faith to stop the fiery arrows of the devil.

**Put on** salvation as your helmet, and take the sword of the Spirit, which is the Word of God.

Pray in the Spirit at all times and on every occasion.

Stay alert and be persistent in your prayers for all believers everywhere.

# The Purpose of God's Armor

### The belt of truth

The enemy fights with lies and sometimes his lies sound like the truth. Only God's truth is able to defeat the lies of the enemy. This belt can protect your integrity.

### The breastplate of righteousness

The enemy will attempt to attack you heart – the seat of your emotions, self-worth, and trust. God's breastplate protects your heart. This breastplate can protect your reputation.

### The shoes of peace

The enemy wants you to think that telling others the Good News about Christ Jesus is a worthless and hopeless task. The shoes that God has given you are the motivation to continue to proclaim true peace that is available in God. To guide your steps.

### The shield of faith

The enemy will always attack you in the form of insults, setbacks, and temptations. The shield of faith protects you from the enemy's arrows.   With this shield you will be able to see beyond your circumstances and know that victory is yours.

## The helmet of salvation

The enemy wants you to doubt God, Jesus and your salvation; the helmet will protect your mind from doubting God. This helmet protects your mind from negative thoughts.

## The sword – God's Word

The sword is the only weapon of offense. There are times when you need to take the offensive against the enemy. When you are tempted, you need to trust in the truth of God's Word. This sword grants you power and authority over the enemy.

Note:  Life Application Study Bible, New Living Translation, Tyndale House Publishers, page 2627

# Redemption

## Ephesians 1

I am equipped through Christ with "every spiritual blessing." (v. 3)

I am chosen in Him "before the foundation of the world." (v. 4)

I am regarded as "holy and blameless before Him." (4)

I am adopted through the "kind intention of His will." (v. 5)

I am redeemed and forgiven, "lavished" with grace (vv. 7-8)

I am a recipient of a glorious "inheritance" in heaven. (v. 11)

I am secured forever by "the Holy Spirit of promise." (vv. 13-14)

I receive a "spirit of wisdom" from the Father (v. 17)

I will be enlightened to grasp the "hope of His calling" (v. 18)

I recognize the "riches of the glory of His inheritance" (v. 18)

I know the "surpassing greatness of His power" toward us (v. 19)

I realize that I am "seated with Christ in heavenly places" (v. 20)

# Knowing Who You Are in Christ JESUS

(Say these out loud & embrace God's truth about you)

It's important to know who you are and whose you are when you approach the throne of God in prayer.

## I AM ACCEPTED

I have been adopted as God's child
Ephesians 1:5

I am God's child
John 1:12

I am Christ's friend
John 15:15

I have been justified
Romans 5:2

I am united with the Lord, and I am in one spirit with Him
1st Corinthians 6:17

I have been bought with a price and I belong to God
1st Corinthians 6:20

I am a member of Christ Jesus' body
1st Corinthians 12:27

I am a saint
Ephesians 1:1

I have direct access to God through the Holy Spirit
Ephesians 2:18

I have been redeemed and forgiven of all my sins
Colossians 1:14

I am complete in Christ
Colossians 2:10

# I AM SECURE

I am free from condemnation
Romans 8:1

I am assured that all things work together for good
God never makes mistakes
Romans 8:28

I cannot be separated from the love of God
Romans 8:35

I have been established, anointed and sealed by God
2nd Corinthians 1:21
I am hidden with Christ in God
Colossians 3:3

I am confident that the good work that God has begun
in me will be perfected
Philippians 1:6

I am a citizen of Heaven
Philippians 3:20

I have not been given a spirit of fear,
but of power, love and of a sound mind
2nd Timothy 1:7

I can find grace and mercy in time of need
Hebrews 4:16

I am born of God and the evil one cannot touch me
1st John 5:18

# I AM SIGNIFICANT

I am the salt and light of the earth
Matthew 5: 13-14

I am a branch of the true vine, a channel of His life
John 15:1-5

I have been chosen and appointed to bear fruit
John 15:16

I am a personal witness of Christ Jesus
Acts 1:8

I am God's temple
1st Corinthians 3:16

I am a minister of reconciliation for God
2nd Corinthians 5:17

I am God's coworker
1st Corinthians 3:9

I am seated with Christ Jesus in the heavenly realm
Ephesians 2:6

I am God's workmanship
Ephesians 2:10

I may approach God with freedom and confidence
Ephesians 3:12

I can do all things through Christ who strengthens me
Philippians 4:13

# Count Your Blessings!

(Past, Present, and Future)

Let all that I am praise the LORD;
With my whole heart, I praise His holy name.

Let all that I am praise the LORD;
May I never forget the good things He does for me.

He forgives all my sins
And He heals all my diseases.

He redeems me from death
And crowns me with love and tender mercies.

He fills my life with good things.
My youth is renewed like the eagle!

Psalm 103:1-5

# An Urgent Prayer

When you are short on time & long on need


*Please, God, rescue me!*
*Come quickly, LORD, and help me.*


*May those who try to harm me*
*Be humiliated and put to shame.*


*May those who take delight in my trouble*
*Be turned back in disgrace.*


*Please hurry to my aid, O God.*
*You are my Helper and my Savior;*
*O LORD, do not delay.*


Psalm 70

# Thankful Praise

*I give thanks to the LORD, for He is good!*
*His faithful love endures forever.*

*I give thanks to God alone, He does mighty miracles.*
*His faithful love endures forever.*

*He made the heavens so skillfully.*
*His faithful love endures forever.*

*He placed the earth among the waters.*
*His faithful love endures forever.*

*He made the heavenly lights.*
*His love endures forever.*

*The sun to rule the day,*
*His faithful love endures forever.*

*And the moon and stars to rule the night.*
*His faithful love endures forever.*

*He remembers me in my weakness.*
*His faithful love endures forever.*

*He saved me from my enemies.*
*His faithful love endures forever.*

*He gives food to every living thing.*
*His faithful love endures forever.*

*I give thanks to the God of heaven.*
*His faithful love endures forever.*

Psalm 136

# Prayer is a Privilege

*O, LORD, hear me as I pray;*
*Pay attention to my groaning.*

*Listen to my cry for help, my King and my God,*
*For I pray to no one but You.*

*Listen to my voice in the morning, LORD.*
*Each morning I bring my request to you and wait*
*expectantly.*

Psalm 5:1-3

# The Prayer of Jabez

This is a very short and powerful prayer, this one verse of prayer that you can personalize. Jabez prayed this prayer and you can too.

*Oh, that You would bless me indeed!*
(You desire **the blessing**)

*Enlarge my territory,*
(You desire **the power and anointing** in your work)

*Please be with me in all that I do,*
(You desire God's hand upon you – **the signature**)

*And keep me from all trouble and pain.*
(You desire God to protect you at all times – **the shielding**)

*And God granted him his request.*

(God supplies all that you need and He answers your prayers)

God supplies because He's **the Supplier**!

1st Chronicles 4:10 NLT

# Beyond Survival

*"Blessed is the one who trusts in the LORD, whose confidence is in Him.*

*They will be like a tree planted by the water that sends out its roots by the stream. It does not fear when heat comes; its leaves are always green. It has no worries in a year of drought and never fails to bear fruit."*

*Jeremiah 17:7-8*

It's a dangerous thing when you turn your heart away from God. All of us experience disappointing circumstances but it's in those very moments that you must turn to God and not away from Him. Have you ever noticed people who lose loved ones and they blame God and get angry with God? If the attitude of that heart is not changed, it can quickly turn to bitterness. Don't lose sight of God in the midst of misfortune. God is mightier than any storm in your life.

In that same chapter *the LORD says: "Cursed are those who put their trust in mere humans, who rely on human strength and turn their hearts from the LORD. They are like stunted shrubs in the desert, with no hope for the future. They will live in the barren wilderness."*

*Jeremiah 17:5-6*

In this passage of Scripture two kinds of people are being contrasted here: those who trust in human beings and those who trust in the Lord. In times of trouble, people who trust in human beings will end up impoverished and spiritually weak. Those who trust in the Lord will flourish like trees planted along a riverbank. While we need positive, viable relationships with others, we are called to seek God first, especially in the midst of a crisis. God wants you to be fruitful not only for your own needs but also to be able to help others. Barren trees produce no fruit. But think about a tree that bears much fruit, many people are able to receive from that tree. Now think of yourself as a tree, will you be like a barren tree or do you see yourself fruitful and flourishing?

Tumbleweeds and trees both have roots. Tumbleweeds, however, don't stay connected to their life-source, they are detached and because of that, they dry out and die. Trees on the other hand, remain connected to their roots, enabling them to flourish and thrive, anchored to that which will sustain them in times of difficulty.

When you stay connected to God, He will strengthen you with the wisdom He speaks in the Bible. And when you talk to Him in prayer, He will give you life-sustaining nourishment that only He can provide.

As a fruitful tree, God will sustain you in times of drought, any crisis in your life won't be able to take you out because your roots run deep in your relationship with the Lord. If you don't stay in His presence, you cannot grow or bear fruit.

# Stay Connected

As you read what Jesus is saying here, I want you to see how important it is that you remain in Him at all times. Jesus is the source of life. You need Him to survive!

Jesus says, *"I am the True Vine, and my Father is the Gardener.*

*Any branch in Me that does not bear fruit [that stops bearing] He cuts away (trims off, takes away); and He cleanses and repeatedly prunes every branch that continues to bear fruit, to make it bear more and richer more excellent fruit.*

*You are cleansed and pruned already, because of the word which I have given you [the teachings I have discussed with you].*

*Dwell in Me, and I will dwell in you. [Live in Me, and I will live in you.] Just as no branch can bear fruit of itself without abiding in (being vitally united to) the vine, neither can you bear fruit unless you abide in Me.*

*I am the Vine; you are the branches. Whoever lives in Me and I in him bears much (abundant) fruit. However, apart from Me [cut off from vital union with Me] you can do nothing.*

*If a person does not dwell in Me, he is thrown out like a [broken-off] branch, and withers; such branches are gathered up and thrown into the fire, and they are burned.*

*If you live in Me [abide vitally united to Me] and My words remain in you and continue to live in your hearts, ask whatever you will, and it shall be done for you.*

*When you bear (produce) much fruit, My Father is honored and glorified, and you show and prove yourselves to be true followers of Mine.*

*John 15:1-8 AMP*

Think about this. You have a partnership with God, which means that there is responsibility on both ends. Your part is to lean on and fully trust in Him. His part is to help you to do what He has assigned you to do in the earth. When you become self-reliant, you are saying, "I don't need God's help, I got this." Things don't work properly in your life unless you invite God into everything you are involved in, His presence makes:

> ➢ the impossible – possible
> ➢ hard things – easy
> ➢ frustrating things – peaceful

Cultivate a flourishing relationship with God by spending time in prayer, reading and studying His Word (the Holy Bible). You cannot do anything of real value without God's help. When you do things of real value, it transforms your life into that abundantly fruitful tree that leaves a lasting legacy.

# Confidence

> *"Come boldly (confidently) to the throne of grace, there you will receive His mercy, and you will find grace to help you when you need it most."*
> Hebrews 4:16

Prayer is a privilege. I am repeating this to help you realize just how special you are to the One who created you. God invites us to come to His throne to have a personal relationship with Him and fellowship daily. Prayer is your approach to God. Do you approach God with your head hung low, afraid to ask Him to meet your needs? Maybe you've come to God with a disrespectful attitude, giving little thought to what you are saying to Him?

We approach God with reverence, highly respecting Him because He is our King. Though at the same time, He wants you to come with bold assurance knowing that He is also your Friend and Counselor.

It's important to know the answers to these questions, because it  will determine how you approach Him. How do you see God?  Who is He to you? Who do you say He is to others?

When you pray, the first things that should come to your mind are:

➢ You belong to God.
➢ The blood of Jesus has cleansed you from all sin.
➢ Because of that blood, you stand before God in His righteousness.
➢ Jesus died your death so you can experience His life.
➢ In Him you qualify for every promise and blessing.

Express your confidence in Jesus! He is the only perfect sacrifice. Worthy is the Lamb of God. You may have messed up and made mistakes, but remember, He is worthy. Remember what He has done for you and rejoice in your new identity in Him. Your confidence can be found in Him.

You can come confidently and approach God as **your Father**. You can come confidently to God as a Friend. And you can come to Him knowing that He is the Righteous Judge that will keep order. He is the Ruler of Heaven and Earth and He has all power. Nothing happens without His knowledge. God is in control!

Jesus said to the followers, *"This is how you should pray:*
*Father, we pray that Your name will always be kept holy.*
*We pray that Your kingdom will come.*
*Give us the food we need for each day.*
*Forgive our sins, just as we forgive everyone who has done*
*wrong to us.*

*And don't let us be tempted."*

Luke 11:2-4 ERV

When you come to God as **Friend**, you know that you can make your petitions known to Him. You can even come to Him on behalf of an earthly friend. Someone may come to you and ask you to pray for them, they may have a need and you will intercede for that person by taking their need (in prayer) to the only One that is able to fulfill that need because God has all of the resources. You are connected to that person and you are connected to God. You are the person in the middle, the intercessor. Not only do you stand on behalf of that person, but you are also standing in agreement with the person.

The word **intercede** means to stand between parties with a view to reconcile differences; to mediate; intervene; to act or interpose in behalf of someone in difficulty or trouble, as by pleading a petition.
(dictionary.com)

# Relationship

*"So you have not received a spirit that makes you fearful slaves. Instead you received God's Spirit when He adopted you as His children. Now we call Him, "Abba Father."*
*Romans 8:15*

We can go to our Father, our Daddy God and ask Him for whatever we need and want. Although He clearly knows what His children need and He abundantly supplies all of that and more. If you grew up without a father in the home or if an abusive father raised you – the concept of a loving father may be strange to you. Let me assure you that our Heavenly Father cannot be compared in any way to earthly fathers. Earthly fathers are limited in their ability to love, but our Heavenly Father is the very essence of love because He is love and He's a giver of love.

> *"Dear friends, we should love each other, because love comes from God. Everyone who loves has become God's child. And so everyone who loves knows God. Anyone who does not love does not know God."*
>
> 1st John 4:7-8

# This Is What Love Looks Like

Love endures and is patient.

Love is kind.

Love is never envious nor boils over with jealousy.

Love is not boastful or vainglorious.

Love does not display itself haughtily.

Love is not conceited (arrogant and inflated with pride).

Love is not rude (unmannerly) and does not act unbecomingly.

Love does not insist on its own rights or its own way, or it is not self-seeking; it is not touchy or fretful or resentful.

Love takes no account of the evil done to it [it pays no attention to a suffered wrong].

Love does not rejoice at injustice and unrighteousness, but rejoices when right and truth prevail.

Love bears up under anything and everything that comes.

Love is ever ready to believe the best of every person.

Love hopes and it's fadeless under all circumstances.

Love endures everything [without weakening].

Love never fails [never fades out or becomes obsolete or comes to an end].

1st Corinthians 13:4-8
AMP Classic

# Your Perfect Prayer Partner

*"[Jesus] is at the right hand of God and is also interceding for us."*

Romans 8:34

You never pray alone, because Jesus is praying for you. He hears you when you pray and He speaks to the Father on your behalf. Your words don't have to be eloquent, just come to Him as you are. He understands you better than anyone else.

*"We do not know what we ought to pray for, but the Spirit himself intercedes for us through wordless groans."*

Romans 8:26

The Son and the Spirit help you when you pray. This should encourage you to continually get in that place of prayer, knowing that your prayer partner is there with you, interceding on your behalf. You are not alone!

Always invite the Holy Spirit into whatever you are going through. He is the Perfect Gentleman, and will never force His way in!

I like what Jennifer Eivaz says in her book,

> *You see, too many people misunderstand who the Holy Spirit is largely due to a lack of teaching. Many think of Him as a force or an "It." Or they pursue just the benefits of the Holy Spirit, such as supernatural power and anointing, without pursuing a relationship with the Person of the Holy Spirit. He is a Person. He is God. He has a personality, intelligence, will and feelings. When we honor Him and lovingly acknowledge Him, He will respond with His Presence.*

*Note: Glory Carriers, Eivaz, Jennifer, Published by Chosen Books, 2019, p. 26*

# Understanding Who God Is

*"Let us make mankind in our image ..."*

Genesis 1:26

The Bible clearly teaches that there is only one God, one essence in three Persons. He is a triune God: God the Father, God the Son, and God the Holy Spirit. Father, Son, and Spirit – they are all God, one divine being expressed as three different personalities. He is One God in three Persons – the Holy Trinity.

When I taught this to young listeners, to help them understand this, I would always use myself as a tangible example by saying: "I am a wife, I am a mother, and I am a teacher. I'm one person, but I function in three different capacities."

*Jesus said, "I and My Father are one."*

John 10:30

Before Jesus left the earth, He promised to send the Holy Spirit.

*"And I will ask the Father, and He will give you another advocate to help you and be with you forever – the Spirit of truth."*

John 14:16-17

# Your Constant Helper

*"Do you not know that your bodies are temples of the Holy Spirit?"*

1st Corinthians 6:19

The Holy Spirit is always present for believers because He dwells in us.

Think about this:

The birth of Jesus – God with us

The death and resurrection of Jesus – God for us

The Holy Spirit – God in us

God loves mankind so much that He did all of this for us, for you, for me, for all of mankind that will accept and believe in His Only Begotten Son Jesus.

*"Yes, God loved the world so much that He gave His Only Son (Christ Jesus), so that everyone who believes in Him would not perish, but can have eternal life."*

John 3:16

The Holy Spirit will dwell within you once you make Jesus the Lord of your life. The Holy Spirit then takes up residence within you and He can turn your physical body into His dwelling place when you are surrendered to Him. You will flow with the power that He gives. You can become a vessel formed for God to use.

# A Special Prayer Language

*"For if I pray in tongues, my spirit prays,*
*but my understanding is unfruitful."*

*1ˢᵗ Corinthians 14:14*

My personal experience with this began many years ago, there was a television preacher teaching about praying in tongues and he simply said, "Ask God to give you this gift. Open up your mouth and begin to praise God continuously. Allow the Holy Spirit to take over your tongue. It will sound like gibberish at first, but keep doing this every day to develop your prayer language." He also said, "Do not be afraid, because although you don't understand what you are saying, something greater than you is occurring in the spirit realm." I began to study this special prayer language for myself, because I wanted to learn more about this great gift that Holy Spirit gives. Wow!

One morning, I actually asked God to give me this special gift and to teach me how to use it. I believe in my heart that anything we ask God for that involves His kingdom coming to earth, that He will equip His children with it; especially if you are mature enough to walk in it. At this point, I had already established a daily routine of waking up early and praying and reading my Bible. I simply asked God to give me this gift. I closed my eyes and I just began to open my mouth and praise Him and worship Him for Who He is. Moments later, I began hearing sounds coming from my mouth that I was not familiar with. I kept my eyes closed and just released my tongue and allowed the words to flow freely. You can do the same, ask Holy Spirit to give you this gift.

Everyone has their own account of how they received this special prayer language. I simply believe that when you accept Jesus Christ as your Lord and Savior, you should also get baptized in the Holy Spirit. I grew up in a Baptist church and we were not taught about getting baptized in the Holy Spirit. I was water baptized at the age of twelve and that was it. Later as I began to hunger and thirst for more of God, that's when He sent teachings my way regarding baptism of the Holy Spirit and speaking in tongues.

Two authors that I admire and who teach clearly on this, I want to share a quote from their books:

*"When you become baptized in the Holy Spirit, you will speak in a brand-new language; only it is a heavenly language, not a natural one. Other terms for the same experience include praying in the Spirit, speaking in an unknown tongue, and receiving the promise of the Father. These terms are mentioned interchangeably in the book of Acts."*

Jennifer Eivaz

*Glory Carriers*

I also like the way Dr. Bill Hamon describes this special language:

*"When we pray in tongues our praying originates and flows from our inner spirit and not from our natural mind. It is not a learned language, but a gift from the Holy Spirit. The natural mind does not understand it."*

Note: Jennifer Eivaz, Glory Carriers, (Chosen Books, 2019), 19
Bill Hamon, Seventy Reasons for Speaking in Tongues, (Destiny Image, 2012), 70

*"Likewise the Spirit also helps in our weaknesses. For we do not know what we should pray for as we ought, but the Spirit Himself makes intercession for us with groaning which cannot be uttered.*

*Now He who searches the heart knows what the mind of the Spirit is, because He makes intercession for the saints according to the will of God."*

Romans 8:26-27

As a believer, you are not left to your own resources to cope with problems. Even when you don't know the right words to pray, the Holy Spirit prays with and for you, and God answers. With God helping you pray, you don't need to be afraid to come before Him. Ask Holy Spirit to intercede for you. When you bring your request to God, trust that He will always do what is best.

# The BLESSING

Numbers 6:24-26

## THE LORD BLESS YOU ...

*May YHWH (HE who exists) kneel before you (making Himself available to you as your HEAVENLY FATHER) so HE can bestow upon you, His promises and gifts.*

## AND KEEP YOU ...

*And GUARD YOU with a HEDGE of THORNY PROTECTION that will prevent Satan and all your enemies from harming you. May HE protect your body, soul, mind, and spirit, your loved ones and all your possessions.*

## THE LORD MAKE HIS FACE SHINE
## UPON YOU ...

*May YHWH (HE who exists) illuminate the WHOLENESS of HIS BEING toward you, continually bringing to order, so that you will fulfill your God-given destiny and purpose.*

## AND BE GRACIOUS TO YOU ...

*May YHWH (HE who exists) provide you with PERFECT LOVE and FELLOWSHIP (never leaving you) and give you SUSTENANCE (provision) and FRIENDSHIP.*

## THE LORD LIFT HIS CONTENANCE ON YOU ...

*May YHWH (HE who exists) LIFT UP and carry His FULLNESS of being toward you (bringing everything that He has to your aid) supporting YOU*

## AND GIVE YOU PEACE ...

*May YHWH (HE who exists) set in place all YOU need to be WHOLE and COMPLETE so you can walk in victory, moment by moment, by the power of the Holy Spirit. May HE give you supernatural health, peace, welfare, safety, soundness, tranquility, prosperity, perfection, fullness, rest harmony, as well as, the absence of agitation and discord.*

*Note: www.WarrenMarcus.com*

# Fearless Faith

Lord, you are my Light and my Savior,
So why should I be afraid of anyone?
The Lord is where my life is safe, so I will be afraid of no one!

Evil people might attack me. They might try to destroy my body. Yes, my enemies might attack me and try to destroy me, but they will stumble and fall.

Even if an army surrounds me, I will not be afraid. Even if people attack me in war, I will trust in the Lord.

I ask only one thing from the LORD. This is what I want most: Let me live in the LORD's house all my life, enjoying the Lord's beauty and spending time in His palace.

He will protect me when I am in danger. He will hide me in His tent. He will take me up to His place of safety.

If He will help me defeat the enemies around me, I will offer sacrifices in His tent with shouts of joy. I will sing and play songs to honor the LORD.

LORD, hear my voice. Be kind and answer me. My heart told me to come to you, LORD, so I am coming to ask for your help.

Don't turn away from me. Don't be angry with me. You are the only one who can help me. My God, don't leave me all alone. You are my Savior.

Even if my mother and father leave me, the LORD will take me in.

I have enemies, LORD, so teach me Your ways. Show me the right way to live.

My enemies have attacked me. They have told lies about me and have tried to hurt me.
But I really believe that I will see the LORD's goodness before I die.

Wait for the LORD's help. Be strong and brave, and wait for the LORD's help.

Psalm 27 ERV

# You Are Healed!

*"By His stripes we are healed."*

---

*"Christ Jesus was being punished for what we did. He was crushed because of our guilt. He took the punishment we deserved, and brought us peace. We were healed because of His pain."*

Isaiah 53:5

---

Sickness and disease will come, but it does not have to remain in your body. When Jesus suffered, bled and died on the cross, His back was brutally beaten for your healing. Receive the healing that He suffered for you to have. Some sickness is unto death, and only God knows why. But other times, the devil could be attacking your body through that sickness and disease. And if that is the case, you must fight with the sword (the Word of God) and make sure you have on the whole armor that God gave you to put on.

During this crucial time of battle, you must not give the enemy any access into your life by speaking words of doubt or fear. This is the time to be on guard with everything you do and say. This may also be a time of fasting and prayer. Some things only come by fasting and praying, therefore you must be willing to turn down your physical plate and feast on the Word of God to strengthen your spirit, soul and your body.

Let your daily prescription be to meditate on God's Word. There are no side effects and you cannot overdose on the Word of God. Most importantly, it may be time to close the door to unhealthy eating and start exercising regularly. Just a short walk can give a tremendous amount of strength to your body each day. If you can, get up and move! Some of God's promises are conditional, meaning you have a part to play; there is something you must do in order for the promises to be released.

I'm speaking from experience, because God has healed my body on more that one occasion. During a time of fasting and praying and reading God's Word, speaking healing Scriptures aloud, and a lifestyle change. God healed my body! Though God is a God of healing I still would encourage you to get your follow-up exams and know your medical numbers for your blood pressure, blood sugar, and even blood tests. Our part is to take care of our bodies. You can't mistreat your body and then expect it to function properly. You want it to last for many years. And most importantly you want to have the good healthy quality of life that Christ Jesus came to give you.

If there is something that you can change or something that can be reversed by a lifestyle change, then by all means do whatever you need to do to maintain good health. Some people live to eat and become overweight, when actually we are supposed to eat to live. For many eating the wrong food and too much of it contributes to health issues. The world has a phrase "comfort food." This is defined as food that provides consolation or a feeling of well being, and most comfort foods contain high amounts of fats, sugars and carbohydrates. Refuse to find comfort in food, instead find comfort in the Comforter (Holy Spirit) especially when you feel like emotional binge eating. You are what you eat! Self -control is a fruit of the Spirit!

"Let food be thy medicine and medicine be thy food."

Hippocrates

My body is the temple of the Holy Spirit (1st Corinthians 6:19)

I discipline my body and keep it under control (1st Corinthians 9:27)

Temperance = self-control

This is a fruit of the Spirit (Galatians 5:23)

# A Prayer for Healing

Father, in the name of Jesus, I confess Your Word concerning healing.

You sent Your Word to heal and deliver us from destruction. I praise and thank You that I am healed, delivered and set free. I repent of any unconfessed sin and receive Your forgiveness.

*I thank and praise You Lord that You are the same yesterday, today and forever.*

Hebrews 13:8

*Even if everyone else is a liar, God will always do what He says.* I totally trust You Lord.

Romans 3:4

As I do this, I believe, *"Your Word will not return to You void, but will accomplish what it says it will."*

Isaiah 55:11

*I believe in the name of Jesus that I am healed.*
Jesus paid for my healing, so I'm walking in health.

1st Peter 2:24

*It is written in Your Word that Jesus himself took our infirmities and bore our sicknesses.*

Matthew 8:17

I am *redeemed from the curse of sickness,* and I refuse to tolerate any symptoms. I declare and decree that every part of my body functions perfectly.

Galatians 3:13

*I submit myself to God. I resist the devil therefore he must flee from me.*

James 4:7

I belong to Almighty God, and I give no place in me to the enemy. *I dwell in the secret place of the Most High God. I abide, remain stable and fixed under the shadow of the Almighty, whose power no foe can withstand.*

Psalm 91:1

*No evil shall befall me, and no plague or calamity shall come near my dwelling.*

Psalm 91:10

I confess that the Word of God abides in me and delivers to me perfect soundness of mind and wholeness in body and spirit. Your Word is medication and life to my flesh for *the law of the Spirit of life operates in me and makes me free from the law of sin and death.*

Romans 8:2

*I have on the whole armor of God, and the shield of faith protects me from all the fiery darts of the wicked.*

Ephesians 6:11,16

Jesus is the High Priest of my confession, and I hold fast to my confession of faith in Your Word. I stand immovable and fixed in full assurance that I have health and healing now in the name of Jesus.

Hebrews 4:14

*My heart is fixed, trusting in the LORD.*

Psalm 112:7

I am submitted to the Word of God

And I believe I am healed

In Jesus' name.

Amen.

# Remain Well!

*"Death and life are in the power of the tongue,*
*and those who love it will eat its fruit."*
*Proverbs 18:21*

Healing already belongs to you! God created your body to heal itself. With God's help, your faith, and you confessing God's Word daily, you can be healed from sickness and disease. Jesus paid for you to be healed of every sickness and disease, every plague and virus – no matter what it is. Do you believe this?

When you read about people that Jesus healed, in many instances their faith played a major role. Do you have faith to receive your healing?

The Lord answered, 'If you had faith even as small as a mustard seed, you could say to this mulberry tree, "May you be uprooted and be planted in the sea," and it would obey you!'

Luke 17:6 NLT

You can say to that sickness or disease in your body, "Be uprooted! In Jesus' Name!" And it will have to obey you, because God has given you the name of Jesus and He has given you the authority to speak His Word.

Jesus says, *"Whatever you forbid on earth will be forbidden in heaven, and whatever you permit on earth will be permitted in heaven."*

Matthew 18:18 NLT

Don't own the sickness or disease by saying, "My (whatever the name of the sickness or disease is)." No! Sickness and disease does not belong to you, it's from the enemy (the thief), he is trespassing and you need to put him out by declaring the Word of God. If you are too weak to pray for yourself, then ask others to pray for you. Prayers of agreement are very powerful!

Jesus says, "The thief's purpose is to steal, kill and destroy. My purpose is to give life in all its fullness."

*John 10:10*

Jesus says, "*If two of you on earth agree on anything you pray for, my Father in heaven will do what you ask.*

*Matthew 18:19 ERV*

Healing belongs to you as a child of God. Jesus purchased *your* healing (make it personal) when He was wounded on the cross. All you have to do is receive it! When His words from the Bible sink down into your heart, His life will bubble up inside of you and it will be like medicine for your body. Make His Word real in your spirit even before you see the healing in your body. Believe His Word and receive your healing!

*"Jesus personally carried our sins in His body on the cross so that we can be dead to sin and live for what is right. By His wounds you are healed."*

1st Peter 2:24 NLT

*"God spoke the words 'Be healed,' and we were healed, delivered from death's door!"*

Psalm 107:20 TPT

*"For with God nothing will be impossible."*

Luke 1:37 NKJV

*"Jesus replied, 'Let the faith of God be in you! Listen to the truth I speak to you: If someone says to this mountain with great faith and having no doubt, "Mountain be lifted up and thrown into the midst of the sea, and believes that what he says will happen, it will be done."*

Mark 11:22-23 TPT

That mountain can be classified as sickness or disease, and by your faith, that mountain can be lifted up out of your life and thrown into the midst of the sea.

*"Now faith brings our hopes into reality and becomes the foundation needed to acquire the things we long for. It is all the evidence required to prove what is still unseen."*

*Hebrews 11:1 TPT*

The things that you have confident faith in - it will develop and be birthed (become a reality). Think about things that are birthed, it's usually a specific time period unknown to you. When a pregnant women is awaiting the birth of her baby, she is excited and expecting great things surrounding the birth of the baby; but she does not know the exact timing that the baby will be birthed yet she waits in joyful anticipation and  is preparing for the birth. As you wait for your healing process to manifest in your physical body, stay in expectation of what God is capable of doing. Nothing is too hard for Him!

➢ If you have a loved one that is sick and they are not able to speak, make it a priority to find healing Scriptures to speak over them. Try not to repeat any negative reports that doctors may give. Listen and in your prayer time. You know what your prayer assignment is, to come against those negative reports using God's Word.

➢ If you are able to visit your loved one, take music and allow praise and worship to saturate the hospital room day and night. Set it on repeat and leave it playing softly next to their bedside when you leave.

➢ Read healing scriptures to them as you sit at their bedside.

➢ No negative talk allowed in the presence of your loved one. Although they may be unconscious, they may be able to hear the conversations around them. No negativity allowed!

➢ Anoint them with anointing oil and pray God's Word over them.

➢ If they are able, take Holy Communion with your loved one.

# Prosperity Promises

*"Beloved friend, I pray that you are prospering in every way and that you continually enjoy good health, just as your soul is prospering."*

3rd John 1:2

The LORD will command the blessing upon all that I set my hands to.

Deuteronomy 28:8

*"Shout in celebration of praise to the Lord! Everyone who loves the Lord and delights in Him will cherish His words and be blessed beyond measure. Great blessing and wealth fills the house of the wise."*

Psalm 112:1,3

*"A good man leaves an inheritance to his children's children: and the wealth of the wicked is treasured up for the righteous."*

Proverbs 13:22

*"In the house of the righteous is much treasure."*

Proverbs 15:6

By humility and fear of the LORD are riches, and honor, and life.

Proverbs 22:4

*"Give generously and generous gifts will be given back to you, shaken down to make room for more. Abundant gifts will pour out upon you with such an overflowing measure that it will run over the top! Your measurement of generosity becomes the measurement of your return."*

Luke 6:38

*"This generous God who supplies abundant seed for the farmer, which becomes bread for our meals, is even more extravagant toward you. First He supplies every need, plus more. Then He multiplies the seed as you sow it, so that the harvest of your generosity will grow."*

2nd Corinthians 9:10

*"And don't allow yourselves to be weary or disheartened in planting good seeds, for the season of reaping the wonderful harvest you've planted is coming!"*

Galatians 6:9

TPT

# The 4 P's:

➤ **Provision**
*The LORD protects you and keeps you alive. He gives you prosperity in the land and rescues you from your enemies.*
Psalm 41:2 NLT

➤ **Protection**
*The LORD is your light and your salvation, so why should you be afraid? The LORD is your fortress, protecting you from danger, so why should you tremble.*
Psalm 24:1 NLT

➤ **Peace**
*The LORD gives His people strength. The LORD blesses you with peace.*
Psalm 29:11 NLT

➤ **Power**
Through God's glorious name and His awesome power, you can push through to any victory and defeat every enemy.
Psalm 44:5

> *"Beloved friend, I pray that you are prospering in every way and that you continually enjoy good health, just as your soul is prospering."*
>
> 3rd John 1:2 TPT

# PART 2: PRAYER

# TIME

> " When you lie down, you will not be afraid. When you rest, your sleep will be peaceful. You have no reason to fear a sudden disaster or the destruction that comes to the wicked."

Proverbs 3:24-25

# Always Ready

*"You must be waiting, watching and praying, because no one knows when that season of time will come."*

Mark 13:33

Prayer watches are specific times of the day or night. If you have ever been awakened during the night or are wondering why you are being led to pray at specific times, it is probably because God wants you to pray or intercede for someone. Every prayer watch has a purpose. I heard someone teach on this subject many years ago and it helped me to be more sensitive to those times that I need to get up and pray.

God is calling each of us to be modern-day watchmen
2nd Kings 9:17-18

When you pray for others, your family, your friends, leaders, neighbors, coworkers, employees and employers, the city you live in, and nations around the world, you are standing watch over them. Your prayers matter! Your prayers for them are effective and will get results! When people are in your prayers, they are in your heart or they are on your mind. You come before God on their behalf. Your connection with them, gives you a commitment to pray for them.

I have heard testimonies where a person is prompted in the middle of the night to get up and pray for someone, and at that very hour, the person being prayed for was saved from something that could have been tragic. This is the reason, you must get up and pray, if the Holy Spirit is prompting you to get up then move urgently to obey. Your prayer in the mid-night hours may be just the thing that will protect the person that you are praying for. After you pray for that person and go back to bed, your sleep is much sweeter because you obeyed God.

Matthew 24:43 says, "but know this, if the good man of the house had known in what **watch** the thief would come, he would have watched and would not have suffered his house to be broken up."

# The First Watch
## Evening
## 6:00 pm – 9:00 pm

King David prayed an evening prayer for sanctification and protection:

*"Please, Lord, come close and come quickly to help me!*
*Listen to my prayer as I call out to You.*

*Let my prayer be as the evening sacrifice that burns like fragrant incense, rising as my offering to you as I lift up my hands in surrendered worship!*

*God, give me grace to guard my lips from speaking what is wrong.*

*Guide me away from temptation and doing evil. Save me from sinful habits and from keeping company with those who are experts in evil. Help me not to share in their sin in any way.*

*When one of Your godly lovers corrects me or one of Your faithful ones rebuke me, I will accept it like an honor I* cannot refuse. It will be healing medicine that I swallow without an offended heart. Even if they are mistaken, I will continue to pray.

When leaders and judges are condemned, falling upon the rocks of justice, then they'll know my words to them were true!

Like an earthquake splits open the earth, so the world of hell will open its mount to swallow their scattered bones.

But You are my Lord and my God; I only have eyes for you! I hide myself in You, so don't leave me defenseless.

Protect me! Keep me from the traps of wickedness they set for me.

Let them all stumble into their own traps while I escape without a scratch!"

Psalm 141 TPT

# The Second Watch
## Night
## 9:00 pm – 12:00 am

This is usually bedtime for most people, especially if you are on a routine schedule and you have to rise early the next morning. The Lord will watch over you during the night. Before you lay down to sleep, make sure you give thanks to God for blessing you throughout the day. It is He who gives you life, strength and resources to do the things you need to do and the things you desire to do. May your sleep be sweet! ☺

*"I will bless the LORD who guides me; even at **night** my heart instructs me. I know the LORD is always with me, I will not be shaken, for He is right beside me. No wonder my heart is glad, and I rejoice. My body rest in safety."*

Psalm 16:7-9

*"During the **night**, the Lord said to Gideon, "Get up, go down against the camp, because I am going to give it into your hands."*

Judges 7:9

*"For last night an angel of the God to whom I belong and whom I serve stood beside me …"*

Acts 27:23

# The Third Watch
# Breaking of Day
# 12:00 am – 3:00 am

This watch hour is one of wrestling marked by victory. Thoughts may interrupt your sleep during this watch hour. If you must, get up and pray and receive the victory. Major changes can occur during this watch of the night.

*"And Jacob was left alone; and there he wrestled a man until **the breaking of the day.** And when he saw that he prevailed not against him, he touched the hollow of his thigh; and the hollow of Jacob's thigh was out of joint, as he wrestled with him. The man said to Jacob, "Let me go, for the day breaks. And Jacob said, "I will not let you go, until you bless me."*

Genesis 32:24-26

We often refer to this hour as midnight, and as you can see in this passage of Scripture, victory and change occurred. When you pray and worship the Lord, things begin to shift.

*"But **at midnight** Paul and Silas were praying and singing hymns to God, and the prisoners were listening to them. Suddenly there was a great earthquake, so that the foundations of the prison were shaken; and immediately all the doors opened and everyone's chains were loosed."*

Acts 16:25-26

# The Fourth Watch
# Early Morning
# 3:00 am – 6:00 am

This prayer watch is a time of preparation for your morning. As you get dressed for your day, you must also put on the whole armor of God (Ephesians 6:10-17). Even if prefer praying in the afternoon or evening, I want to encourage you to start your day with prayer. If you pray before your day begins, prayer sets the tone for your entire day and if you seek God early in the morning, He can give you instruction or may even warn you of things that may occur.

*"Then Jacob rose **early in the morning**, and took the stone that he had put at his head, set it up as a pillar, and poured oil on top of it. And he called the name of that place Bethel."*

Genesis 28:18-19

*Early the next morning Jesus stood on the shore. But the disciples did not know it was Jesus. Then He said to them, "Friends, have you caught any fish?"*

*John 21:4-5*

In this passage of Scripture, the disciples had fished all night, but they caught nothing. Jesus met them in their place of frustration, early in the morning, and he gave them a simple instruction and when they obeyed Him; they had more fish than they could haul in. God wants to bless you like that, He wants to give you an Ephesians 3:20 Blessing, early in the morning. Seek Him early in the morning! Seek Him first!

# The Fifth Watch
# Morning
# 6:00 am – 9:00 am

During this prayer watch, sometimes, you may be most focused on your priorities for the morning. As you prioritize your work duties remember whom you are working for whether you are an employee or an entrepreneur. Who are you working for?

*"In all the work you are given, do the best you can. Work as though you are working for the Lord, rather than for people."*

Colossians 3:23

If you are an entrepreneur, then I want to encourage you to make sure the Lord is the CEO of your business. Meet with God your CEO every day so that He can direct your steps and give you strategies for a successful business. All that you do and all that you are is because of Him!

"And you shall remember the LORD your God, for it is He who gives you power to get wealth."

Deuteronomy 8:18


"For His anger is but for a moment, His favor is for a lifetime. Weeping may endure for a night, but a shout of joy comes in the **morning**."

Psalm 30:5


"Through the Lord's mercies we are not consumed, Because His compassions fail not. They are new every **morning**; Great is Your faithfulness."

Lamentations 3:22-23

# The Sixth Watch
## Day
## 9:00 am – 12:00 pm

This is usually a time of high energy and productivity during this watch of the day. You have prepared and prioritized your activities for the day and now you will implement those things. As you work, pray within. A time of constant communion with God even as you work. He will strengthen you and give you wisdom during this time.

*"Let my mouth be filled with Your praise and with Your glory all the **day**."*
Psalm 71:8

*"Every **day** I will bless You, and I will praise Your name forever and ever."*
Psalm 145:2

Let this be a time of high praise in the midst of busy productivity.

# The Seventh Watch
## Midday
## 12:00 pm – 3:00 pm

The sun is usually at its fullest and brightest during this time of day. Pray that your life would be bright for Christ. Pray not to be led into any temptation, trap, or snare of the enemy.

*"The path of the righteous is like the morning sun, shining ever brighter till the full light of day."*

Proverbs 4:18

*"In the same way, let your light shine before others, that they may see your good deeds and glorify your Father in heaven."*

Matthew 5:16

"At **midday**, O king, along the road I saw a light from heaven, brighter than the sun, shining around me and those who journeyed with me."

Acts 26:13

This was a time of conversion for the Apostle Paul; this journey was life changing for him. As you journey through your day, keep your heart and mind stayed on Christ Jesus and He will guide you every step of the way.

# The Eighth Watch
## Afternoon
## 3:00 pm – 6:00 pm

For most people, this is the ending time of your workday. It's amazing that there are eight watches of the day. The number eight means "new beginnings," and at the end of each day you get to rejoice in all that God has done for you and through you during the day. And by the grace of God, you have a new beginning for each new day. That's why you must live in the present, the gift of today!

At the end of each workday, you have accomplished something. Not only will you receive pay for the time that you have given, but also you should have accomplished something in the place that you invested several hours of your day. Your presence should change the atmosphere that you enter, bringing in the light of Christ Jesus, bringing hope to those around you. Jesus gave you power to live a life of victory and authority to accomplish God's will here on earth. You are co-missioned, meaning your mission is His mission – you are in partnership with Him so that His Kingdom may come and His will be done on earth through you.

*And Jesus came and spoke to them saying, "All authority has been given to Me in heaven and on earth. Go therefore and make disciples of all the nations, baptizing them in the name of the Father and of the Son and of the Holy Spirit, teaching them to observe all things that I have commanded you; and I am with you always, even to the end of the age. Amen.*

Matthew 28:18-20

*"Yet in all these things we are more than conquerors through Him who loved us."*

Romans 8:37

# Disciplines Linked to Your Destiny

In Matthew 6, Jesus teaches us three disciplines that we should partake of. When He teaches about each of these disciplines, He doesn't say *"if,"* He says *"when."* You are expected to discipline yourself to do these things. Jesus gives specific instruction on when you give. He also teaches on when you pray and when to fast. With each of these disciplines, you must check your motives: are you doing any of these to be seen by others? Do you desire the praise of people, or the rewards of God? Always be mindful of the fact that God is looking at your heart. He knows your why for everything that you do.

Each of these disciplines can change the course of your life. Prayer brings you closer to God; it's the greatest intimacy because it goes beyond physical limitation. Fasting humbles you and it can heal your physical body. Giving can break financial lack off of your money. I know of several people whose giving has broken generational financial curses off of their bloodlines. You tithe in obedience to God, you are sowing seed in your giving. What does seed do? It grows into a harvest. And some give alms out of compassion for the poor. Sow your seed into good soil!

*"Honor the LORD with your wealth and with the first fruits of all your crops (income)."* Proverbs 3:9 AMP

# Never Give Up!

*"Ask and it will be given to you; seek, and you will find;*

*knock, and it will be opened to you."*

Matthew 7:7

Someone taught me this many years ago regarding this Scripture: How do you ask? You ask in prayer. How do you seek God? Through fasting and prayer. When you are wholeheartedly seeking God, you will turn down your plate by fasting and praying. Fasting and prayer combined makes you more attentive and sensitive to the things of God. The Word of God becomes your food.

Oftentimes we want God to answer our prayers when and how we want. But it is God Who knows what's best. You must be okay with the fact that God's ways are not your ways and His thoughts are much higher than your mind could ever comprehend (read Isaiah 55:8-9). If you are a parent, then you can relate to this: If your ten year old comes to you and ask for your car keys are you going to give them up? I hope your answer is a solid "No!" Your responsibility is to protect and guide that child. You will know when the time is right as they mature. Some things you ask God for, but it may not be His timing yet. You must be willing to wait on His timing.

Some children are rebellious. If the parent says "No!" or "Not now" a rebellious child will attempt to do whatever to have their way. If you are trying to get around God and do things your way, it usually does not turn out well. Some people have a plan B set up in their mind but God is the only plan. There is no plan B that will work outside of God's will for your life. You must know that His timing is always perfect; He's never late – always on time.

While you are in that place and process of waiting, what should you be doing? Be a good waiter. What do waiters do? They serve others. As you serve others, your blessing will show up in ways you never imagined. It helps to take the focus off of self. You should also remember how God has always shown up in the past; sometimes you have to take a brief walk down memory lane. Don't forget how God has blessed you.

# Journal Your Journey

This is an excellent way to help you to know that God hears and He answers your prayer. Keep a prayer journal. Add the date when you first made your prayer petition known to God. Write out the prayer request in detail, and then list the Scripture that you are standing on as you wait for God. It is important to list a scripture because you must know that what you are praying for is in the Word of God. His will and His promises are in His Word; therefore you should be able to list a scripture next to your prayer request. And here's the best part: when God answers that prayer add that date as well.

Here is what you will discover when keeping a prayer journal, God always answers and He's always on time. He does more than what you were expecting. Some of the things listed in my prayer journal were answered immediately and some were answered months or even years later. Some of those prayers were not answered in the way that I anticipated but guess what? It's okay because I know He heard my prayer, I trust His timing and His Word *never returns void* (read Isaiah 55:11).

This journal helps me to always remember how faithful God is. I want to encourage you to keep a prayer journal. It can become a spiritual legacy for you to leave for future generations. To build their faith in God and so that they can know just how faithful He really is.

# PART 3: BARRIERS THAT BLOCK RESULTS

> *"The little foxes are ruining the vineyards."*
>
> *Song of Solomon 2:15 TLB*

It's the little foxes that spoil the vines of your life. What are some of those secret sins that only you and God know about? There are certain subtle things that can block your prayers from being answered and these are things that you have to deal with. The enemy is always attempting to stop the plans of God, but there are also things that you do that can hinder your prayers, let's look as some of them:

1. **Unforgiveness**

   People will offend you and hurt you, but you must forgive them. This does not excuse what they did, but forgiveness sets you free and keeps you in right relationship with God. Allow God to deal with those that hurt you because they are not getting away with anything.

*"If you forgive other people when they sin against you, your heavenly Father will also forgive you. But if you do not forgive others their sins, your Father will not forgive your sins."*

Matthew 6:14-15

*"When you stand praying, if you hold anything against anyone, forgive them, so that your Father in heaven may forgive you your sins."*

Mark 11:25

## 2. Your Decisions

Too often we choose companions, jobs, houses, new locations and  many other things without seeking God's will. Many times this can lead to endless regrets and severe consequences. Don't rush into anything. Always take time to consult God first.

*"Seek first the kingdom of God ..."*

The Amplified Bible says it this way, *"But first and most importantly seek (aim at, strive after) His kingdom and His righteousness [His way of doing*

*and being right – the attitude and character of God],*
*and all these things will be given to you also."*

Matthew 6:33 AMP


## 3. Hypocrisy

When you tell others that you are a Christian and your deeds do not match your words, you don't represent the Kingdom of God well. People who don't know God may want to know Him, but because of your hypocrisy, they may turn away.


*"So you, also, outwardly seem to be just and upright to men, but inwardly you are full of hypocrisy and lawlessness."*

Matthew 23:28

### 4. Trying to Fit In

Stop trying to fit in when you were born to stand out, to make a difference in the world. If certain people in the world don't accept your Lord and Savior Jesus Christ, then they will not accept you. You be the influence they need, don't allow them to cause you to deny the One that saved you. Don't conform to the world, instead transform and renew your mind.

*"Don't copy the behavior and customs of this world, but be a new and different person with a fresh newness in all you do and think. Then you will learn from your own experiences how His ways will really satisfy you."*

Romans 12:2 TLB

## 5. Selfishness

You are not created to live in a bubble by yourself and care only about what you want and disregard others around you. It's not all about you! It's all about JESUS!

*"In whatever you do, don't let selfishness or pride be your guide. Be humble, and honor others more than yourselves."*

Philippians 2:3

## 6. Being Lukewarm

God wants all of you – not just an hour on Sundays. You are on planet earth for a reason and a season; the most important thing for you to do while you are here is to do God's will for your life. He has a specific purpose for you, and if you don't know what that purpose is then you must find out. Do not put your interests ahead of the purpose that He created you for. You will have to one-day answer to Him and give an account of what you did with the life that He gave you.

*"So because you are lukewarm (spiritually useless), and neither hot nor cold, I will vomit you out of My mouth [rejecting you with disgust]."*

Revelation 3:16 AMP

## 7. Failing to Love Others

If you don't know the love of Christ Jesus, then you really do not know the true meaning of love. *God so loved the world that He gave His only begotten Son Jesus* (John 3:16). And if you truly know the significance of Him dying on the cross then you may have a revelation of what real love is. We are commanded to love God and to love others (Matthew 22:37-40). Everything about Him exemplifies love. If you are a genuine follower of Christ Jesus, then you are equipped to walk in love. John 13:35 says, *"Your love for one another will prove to the world that you are my disciples."*

## 8. Not Praying for Others

Just as you pray for yourself and your loved ones, you should also pray for: pastors, teachers, missionaries, first responders, emergency personnel, and for all those in authority (1st Timothy 2:2). When you do not pray for these people, you not only fail them but you sin against God. You should also pray for the sick, the widow, the orphan, and the lonely that you come in contact with. Even if you know of someone, and you don't know him or her personally, pray for them. 1st Samuel 12:23 says, *"Moreover as for me, God forbid that I should sin against the Lord in ceasing to pray for you."*

## 9. Not Doing Good

We are living in perilous times where the world considers good evil and evil good. This is dangerous because either people are choosing to compromise or just don't care. As Christians, you cannot find yourself in the ways of the world. The Lord has commanded you to do good to all, especially to the household of faith. If you are filled with the Holy Spirit, goodness is a fruit of the Spirit. James 4:17 says, *"Therefore, to him who knows to do good and does not do it, to him it is sin."*

## 10. Anger

It's human nature to get angry occasionally, but do you remain in a nasty attitude of anger, every day? If so, you are playing with a loaded gun and you need to get help immediately. Anger is dangerous because it starts out as a tiny seed of anger, but it can develop into rage and then murder. We see this tragic progression all the time on the bad news media, that's why so many people are in anger management classes, in prison for murder or assault charges and in therapy sessions to help them control their raging anger. You must pray and get rid of that anger immediately, don't allow it to grow in your heart. The Bible tells us in Ephesians 4:26, *"When you are angry, don't let that anger make you sin. And don't stay angry all day."* If you need professional help, then obtain it so that you can become free from those toxic emotions.

# PART 4: SONGS OF PRAISE

# Sing for Joy

During your prayer time, hum or sing a song to God. He loves the sound of your voice. You have an audience of One and as you sing, whatever burdens you were carrying they will begin to lift. Your soul will rise to receive the joy of the Lord.

*"The joy of the Lord is your strength."*

*Nehemiah 8:10*

*"My heart, O God, is quiet and confident, all because of you. Now I can sing my song with passionate praises! Awake, O my soul, with the music of His splendor."*

Psalm 108:1

*"Arise, my soul, and sing His praises! I will awaken the dawn with my worship, greeting the daybreak with my songs of light."*

Psalm 108:2

During some of my early years of early Morning Prayer, when I entered into my prayer time, singing would wake me up and joy would fill my heart almost immediately. Here are some of my favorite songs that I sang and still sing. Believe me when I say, that I'm so happy that our Heavenly Father loves our individual singing voices regardless of how it sounds. Worship music and songs come from a pure place in your heart. Now lift up your voice and sing to the Lord.

# This is the Day

Psalm 118:24

This is the day, this is the day that the Lord has made,
that the Lord has made.
I will rejoice, I will rejoice and be glad in it, and be
glad in it.
This is the day that the Lord has made
and I will rejoice and be glad in it.

I will enter His gates with thanksgiving in my heart,
I will enter His courts with praise,
I will say this is the day that the Lord has made.
I will rejoice for He has made me glad.
He has made me glad, He has made me glad.
I will rejoice for He has made me glad.

*Song written by Matt Johnson*
*Originally released September 1983*

# I'm Available to You

**Verse 1**

You gave me my hands to reach out to man

To show him Your love and Your perfect plan

You gave me my ears, I can hear Your voice so clear

I can hear the cries of sinners

But cannot wipe away their tears

**Verse 2**

You gave me my voice to speak Your Word

To sing all Your praises, to those who never heard

But with my eyes I can see a need for more availability

I've seen the hearts that have been broken

So many people to be free

**Chorus**

Lord, I'm available to You

My will I give to You

I'll do what You say to

Use me Lord to show someone the way and enable me to say,

My storage is empty and I am available to You

**Verse 3**

Now I'm giving back to You all the tools You gave to me

My hands, my ears, my voice, my eyes

So You can use them as You please

I have emptied out my cup so that You can fill me up

Now I'm free, I just want to be more available to You

Original Writer
Unknown

# Amazing Grace

### Verse 1

Amazing grace! How sweet the sound
That saved a wretch like me.
I once was lost, but now am found,
Was blind, but now I see.

### Verse 2

'Twas grace that taught my heart to fear,
And grace my fears relieved.
How precious did that grace appear
The hour I first believed.

### Chorus

(Chris Tomlin and Louie Giglio wrote new chorus 2008)

My chains are gone
I've been set free
My God my Savior
Has ransomed me.
And like a flood
His mercy rains
Unending love,
Amazing Grace.

## Verse 3

The Lord has promised good to me
His Word my hope secures
He will shield and portion be
As long as life endures

## Verse 4

Through many dangers, toils and snares
I have already come;
'Tis grace hath brought me safe thus far
And grace will lead me home.

### Sing Chorus again

*Originally written by*
*John Newton*

This song was written centuries ago, but it remains a timeless classic that has been sung for many generations. The lyrics are powerful. When you sing this song, you will find yourself thanking God for your salvation and all that He does because this song can bring reflection on how merciful God really is and how much He loves you.

# What A Friend We Have In Jesus

What a Friend we have in Jesus,

All our sins and griefs to bear!

What a privilege to carry

Everything to God in prayer!

O what peace we often forfeit,

O what needless pain we bear,

All because we do not carry

Everything to God in prayer!

*Originally written by*
*Joseph M. Scriven*

There are more verses to this song, but this is the one I sing, actually this is the only verse I know ☺

*"I will sing you a new song, O God ..."*
*Psalm 144:9*

If you just don't like singing, then I would suggest that you get some good praise and worship music to listen to because it sets the atmosphere when you are praying. The book of Psalms is filled with lyrics. Open up the Bible and begin to sing the words right out of the pages. I have done this before, and words cannot describe how your spirit rejoices in doing this. Some of you reading this book, you are called to write songs. Write the songs of inspiration that the world needs to hear. Write songs that will transform the hearts of people and set places of praise. Rejoice in the Lord!

# There's Something About That Name

Jesus, Jesus, Jesus

There's something about that name

Master, Savior, Jesus

Like a fragrance after the rain


Jesus, Jesus, Jesus

Let heaven and earth proclaim

Kings and kingdoms will all pass away

But there's something about that name


Author Unknown

*"The LORD your God in your midst, the Mighty One, will save;*

*He will rejoice over you with gladness, He will quiet you with His love,*

*He will rejoice over you with singing."*

*Zephaniah 3:17 NKJV*

## Declare this today:

*"He calms me with His love,*
*And delights me with His songs."*
*MSG*

# ABOUT GENOLIA

*Born to Write*

Genolia began writing poetry at the age of twelve. Years later, she enjoyed being a Feature Writer for her college newspaper. She is a former Educator and during her years in the field of education she wrote plays for students to perform and poetry for them to recite on several occasions. Her love for books and writing is contagious. Genolia serves as an Elder at her church. Every week she prays with many people at the altar and on the streaming Prayer Line. Genolia enjoys teaching Bible study classes. She has plans to write more books to reach people who are looking for positive encouragement. Genolia is a wife and mother and resides in Illinois.

*God speaks in the silence of the heart.*

*Listening is the beginning of prayer.*

*Mother Teresa*

www.ingramcontent.com/pod-product-compliance
Lightning Source LLC
Chambersburg PA
CBHW070806050426
42452CB00011B/1922